This book
belongs
to

Kathmar

Johanna

William

Reprinted 1988 by Macdonald & Co (Publishers) Ltd under
the Black Cat imprint

Macdonald & Co (Publishers) Ltd,
3rd Floor, Greater London House,
Hampstead Road, London NW1 7QX

a member of Maxwell Pergamon Publishing Corporation plc

ISBN 0-7481-0102-9
Printed in GDR

A-Z
OF
NATURE

**Written and illustrated by
Colin and Moira Maclean**

BLACK CAT

Aa

adder
A small venomous snake belonging to the viper family. It has dark zigzag markings.

aestivation
Summer sleep. Many desert animals sleep through the summer's heat.

alga
The simplest kind of plant, without flowers or roots. Seaweeds are algae.

alligator
A large carnivorous reptile found in swamps and rivers in hot climates. It has huge, powerful jaws with many teeth, and a long, heavy tail.

amoeba
A tiny, single-celled animal found in ponds and streams.

amphibian
A cold-blooded vertebrate. It spends the first part of its life in water, the second either in water or on land. Frogs, toads, newts and salamanders are amphibians.

anemone
A flower belonging to the buttercup family. Some anemones are called windflowers, because they tremble in the slightest breeze.

anemone   wood anemone

anglerfish
A fish that catches its prey with the help of a 'fishing-rod' attached to its head. This strange hooked line is actually a part of the dorsal fin. (See **fish**.)

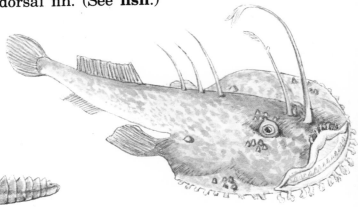

animal
Any living thing that cannot make its own food. A plant can use sun, air and water to make food (see **energy cycle**). It can also draw nourishment from the soil through its roots. An animal cannot do this. It usually has to search for food, so most animals can move around. Animals that cannot move, such as sponges and corals, live in the sea, where they simply catch their food as it drifts past. Insects, fishes, amphibians, reptiles, birds and mammals are all animals which move around.

ant
An insect that lives and works with others of its species in highly-organised colonies (see **social insects**). There are thousands of different species of ants. The biggest, called army or soldier ants, march along in columns eating any other insects in their way. They even eat small birds and mammals.

ant-eater
A mammal that feeds on ants. It has weak teeth and a long tongue.

antelope
A swift-moving mammal with hollow horns. It is a ruminant, related to cattle, sheep and goats.

Thompson's gazelle

impala

ape
A mammal belonging to the order known as primates. Apes are more like human beings than any other animal. They have the same number of teeth, similar hands and can walk upright on their hindlegs. They are also intelligent, although an ape's brain is less than half the size of a human brain. There are four species of ape—the gorilla, the chimpanzee, the orang-utan and the gibbon.

aphid
A small, soft-bodied bug that sucks the juice of plants. Juice that passes through an aphid is called honeydew.

arachnid
An animal with two main parts to its body, and four pairs of legs. Spiders and scorpions are arachnids.

armadillo
The only armoured mammal. Its armour is made of horny plates.

nine-banded armadillo

ass
A long-eared mammal related to the horse. The domestic donkey is an ass.

African wild ass

Bb

baboon

A fierce, powerful monkey that lives on grasslands and hunts in packs. A pack of baboons will even attack a leopard.

badger

A nocturnal mammal with a black and white striped head, related to the stoat and the weasel. It is an expert digger, with strong, short legs and powerful claws.

balance of nature

How all the living things in an environment depend on each other for survival. If any part of an environment is destroyed, or if a species is removed or added, the balance is upset. For instance, if plants are destroyed plant-eaters will die and so will the animals that prey on them. On the other hand, if a species is added to an environment where it has no predators, its numbers will grow rapidly. They will eat up too much of the available food, and other creatures will suffer (see **conservation** and **food chain**).

bamboo

The tallest and thickest grass in the world.

baobab

A huge tree found on hot grasslands. It has a bottle-shaped trunk for storing water.

bark

The protective layer that grows on the outside of tree trunks and shrub stems. Bark keeps moisture in the trunk and protects it from damage by heat, cold and decay.

beak

The horny front part of a bird's head, used as a feeding tool. Birds have different sorts of beaks, depending on the kind of food they eat. Fine beaks can snap up insects, and hooked beaks can tear flesh. Stout beaks crack seeds and nuts, and saw-edged beaks grip slippery fish. Long, slender beaks are needed for drinking nectar.

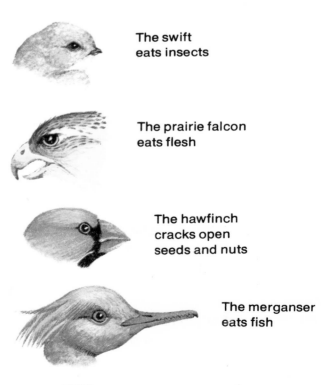

The swift eats insects

The prairie falcon eats flesh

The hawfinch cracks open seeds and nuts

The merganser eats fish

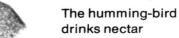

The humming-bird drinks nectar

bear

A heavy mammal with thick fur. Bears are usually slow-moving, but when alarmed or on the attack they can gallop surprisingly fast. They belong to the order of carnivores, but are, in fact, omnivorous. Polar bears are white and live near the North Pole.

beech

A tall tree with smooth, grey bark and dense foliage. Its triangular brown nuts are known as beech-mast.

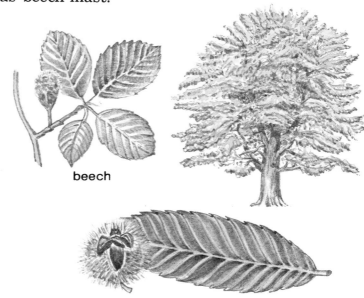

beech

sweet chestnut

beaver

The most intelligent rodent. Beavers build their homes in shallow streams. First they gnaw down trees and dam, or block, the stream to keep the water always at the same level. Then they build a large, solid house called a lodge.

bee

A flying insect that gathers nectar and pollen for its young (see **flower**). When a honey-bee finds a good supply of nectar, it flies back to the hive. There it does a special kind of dance that tells the other bees where the nectar is (see **social insects**).

honey-bee

beetle

An insect that uses only its hindwings for flying. It uses its hard forewings to protect its body.

stag beetle

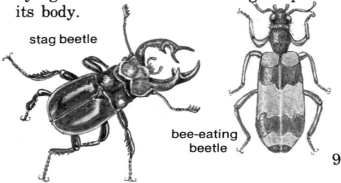

bee-eating beetle

9

biology
The study of life and living things.

bioluminescence
Light produced by living things. Angler-fishes, squid, jellyfishes and many other animals that live in dark parts of the sea can produce light. The firefly and glow-worm, which are nocturnal beetles belonging to the same family, glow brightly during the mating season.

birch
A tree with silvery-white bark. Its twigs are used to make brooms.

bird
A warm-blooded animal with feathers to keep it warm and help it to fly. The main wing feathers give the bird lift, while the large ones at the tips help it to change direction. Tail feathers act as a rudder and a brake. Birds have hollow bones to make them light.

primary feathers

covering feathers

secondary feathers

birds of prey
An order of birds with strong, hooked beaks for tearing flesh.

marsh harrier

sparrowhawk

osprey

gyrfalcon

bison

The largest land animal in America. Bison are a type of cattle found on grasslands, and are also known as buffalo.

bivalve

A water-living mollusc protected by a double shell. It has a foot and can move around, but has no eyes.

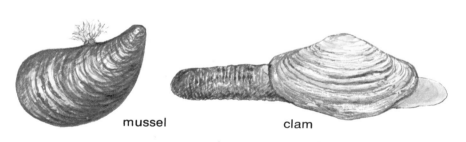

mussel

clam

boa

A non-venomous snake that kills its prey by coiling its body around it and squeezing it to death. Boas and other snakes that do this are called constrictors.

Cook's tree boa

botany

The study of plant life.

broom

A yellow-flowered shrub. Its flowers produce no nectar, but instead spray pollen on to bees.

budgerigar

A small, brightly-coloured bird related to the parrot and found in Australia. It can mimic the human voice and is a popular pet.

bug

An insect that feeds by sucking the juices of plants or the blood of animals.

fire-bug

striped bug

backswimmer

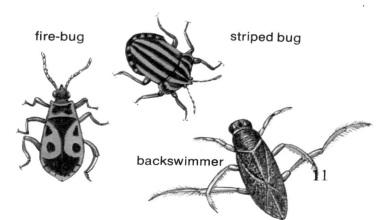

11

bush-baby

A small nocturnal primate that lives in trees. It has huge eyes and silky fur.

buttercup

A yellow flower found in gardens and meadows. Many flowers of different colours belong to the buttercup family, and most of them are poisonous.

meadow
buttercup

water
crowsfoot

butterfly

An insect with large, often brightly-coloured wings. A butterfly's mouth is a long tube for sucking up nectar. When not in use, it is coiled up under the head. (See **metamorphosis**.)

common blue

small tortoiseshell

small heath

Cc

cactus

A spiny plant with no true leaves, found in deserts and other dry places. It can store water in its body, or stem, and so can live for long spells without rain.

camel

A desert-living mammal. The Arabian camel, or dromedary, has one hump, the Bactrian camel has two. Both camels store fat in their humps to give them energy when food is scarce.

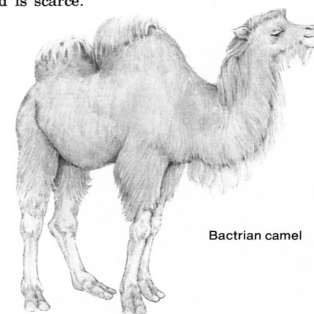

Bactrian camel

camouflage

Protective pattern or colouring that helps an animal to hide from its enemies. Some animals, like chameleons and flat-fishes, can change colour to match different backgrounds. Others disguise themselves as stones, leaves and twigs. Stripes can help by breaking up an animal's outline and making it harder to see.

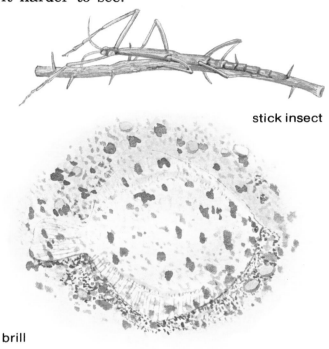

stick insect

brill

cannibal

An animal that eats others belonging to the same species. No animals do this all the time, but some become cannibals if they live in overcrowded conditions.

Arabian camel

carnation

A plant that swells where the flowers or leaves join the stem. The flowers are usually sweet-smelling.

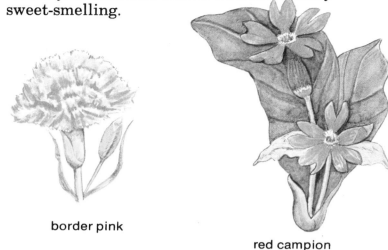

border pink

red campion

carnivore

An animal that eats other animals. There is an order of mammals called carnivores. It includes dogs, cats, bears, weasels, badgers, raccoons, seals and hyenas.

carp

A freshwater fish with toothless jaws. Goldfishes and minnows belong to the carp family.

goldfish

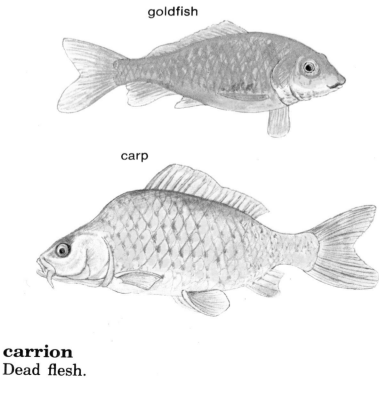

carp

carrion

Dead flesh.

13

cat

A carnivore with very sharp hearing and eyesight. Cats that live in the wild are known as big cats. Some, like the tiger and the lion, are very large indeed, but others, like the American margay and the European wild cat, are much the same size as the domestic cat. The lion lives and hunts in groups called troops but other big cats hunt alone or in pairs, usually at dusk. Domestic cats were kept in China and Egypt thousands of years ago, and were the ancestors of the pets we keep today.

tabby

Persian

lynx

caterpillar

The larva of a butterfly or moth.

puss moth

14

catfish

A fish with whisker-like growths, called barbels, around its mouth.

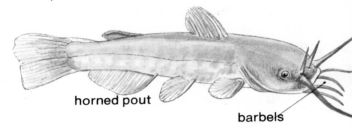

horned pout

barbels

catkin

A cluster of tiny flowers, looking rather like a woolly tail, found on some trees. There are both male and female catkins.

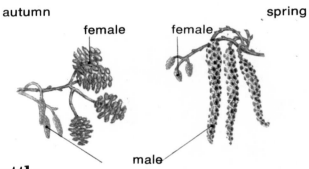

autumn

female

spring

female

male

cattle

Large, horned ruminants. They have always been hunted and farmed for their meat, their milk and their skins. People also use them to pull and carry heavy loads.

domestic cow

yak

cavy

A rodent with small ears and no tail. Wild cavies are found only in South America. The pet guinea pig is a cavy.

guinea pig

cedar

A conifer belonging to the pine tree family. It has a sweet-smelling oil in its wood.

cedar of Lebanon

cell

The basic unit of life, from which all plants and animals are made. Simple animals like the amoeba are made up of only one cell. People are made up of millions of cells.

centipede

A fast-running animal with many legs. Its name means 'a hundred feet'. In fact, some centipedes have more than a hundred, and others less. Centipedes feed on worms and insects, which they catch and poison.

chameleon

A lizard that can move each of its eyes separately. It catches prey by shooting out its long tongue. Chameleons hide from their enemies by changing their colour (see **camouflage**).

cheetah

The fastest runner of the big cats, reaching 112 km per hour. It is quite easily tamed and trained and is often used in hunting antelopes.

chimpanzee

An ape found in Africa. It roams the forest in large groups by day, and at night makes a nest in the trees. Because it is intelligent and inquisitive, the chimpanzee enjoys working with people and learning from them.

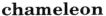

15

chrysalis

The pupa of a butterfly or moth.

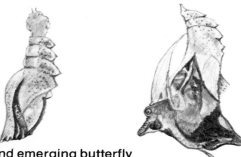

chrysalis and emerging butterfly

cicada

A bug that makes a loud noise by vibrating a pair of drums on its body.

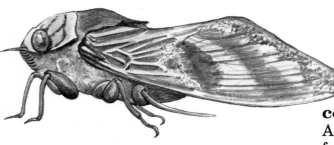

clematis

A climbing plant with wiry stems and feathery seeds. It belongs to the buttercup family.

climate

The pattern of weather in any area over a long period of time.

clover

A plant belonging to the same family as broom. Its flowers form a cluster and its leaves are in three parts. Four-leaved clovers are very rare, and thought to be lucky.

clover

16

cobra

A venomous snake. When alarmed, it raises the ribs near its head. The skin is stretched over them to form a kind of hood.

cocoon

A protective covering. Spiders make cocoons for their eggs. An insect larva often makes a cocoon in which the pupa forms.

opened cocoon
with pupa inside

cod

A sea fish that people have always liked to eat. It feeds mainly on crustaceans, but will eat almost anything—stones, turnips and bottles have been found in cods' stomachs! Many food fishes, such as hake, whiting and haddock, belong to the cod family.

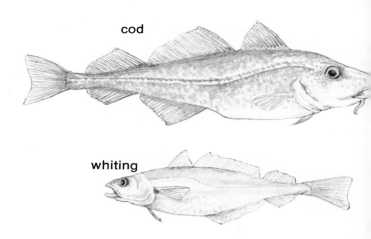

cod

whiting

cold-blooded animal

An animal whose body temperature rises or drops to match the temperature of its surroundings. Insects, reptiles and amphibians are cold-blooded.

communication

Animals can 'talk' to their own kind by using sound, smell, sight and touch. For example, dogs bark, birds sing and catfishes grunt. Whales and dolphins whistle. Many mammals, fishes and insects produce special scents. These can be used to attract their own species, or to warn them of danger. Insects touch each other with their feelers. Birds and mammals groom each other's feathers or fur. All these are ways of communicating.

conifer

A tree with male and female cones. Most conifers have needle-like leaves, and most are evergreen.

coniferous forest

Forest found mainly in cold climates or on mountains. Tough conifer needles are slow to decay and pile up to form a thick carpet on the ground. Not many plants can grow in this, which means there is not much food for animals.

long-eared owl

fallow deer

ground squirrel

fern

crossbill

wood mushroom

Douglas fir

Norway spruce

cedar

red admiral butterfly

bramble

wood sorrel

17

conservation

Making the best use of the world's resources of oil, minerals, plants and animals. We depend upon these for our buildings, transport, fuel and food. For a long time people have been hunting animals, cutting down forests, digging up land, building houses and factories and pouring fumes into the air and waste into seas and rivers. Now we know that doing these things destroys environments and threatens the plants and animals upon which we depend. We try to avoid upsetting the balance of nature by preventing pollution, protecting threatened species and preserving certain areas as national parks and game reserves. (See **balance of nature**.)

coral

A tiny animal with a soft body and a hard skeleton. Corals live in warm seas and usually grow together in colonies. Over many years their skeletons form a large mass called a reef. Coral reefs are a wonderful environment for many plants and animals.

cormorant

A long-necked bird that dives for fish. It belongs to the same order as the pelican. The Chinese train cormorants to fish from boats for them.

shag

cormorant

courtship

How an animal finds a mate. Animals that do not live in groups may have to attract a mate over quite a long distance. Some female fishes and moths do this by releasing a scent. Male salmon and herons prepare a nest to attract the female. Some male spiders dance, while others offer a fly wrapped in silk as a gift. Male mammals often fight, while birds, like the peacock and the bird of paradise, display their brilliant feathers.

crab

A crustacean with large pincers and four pairs of walking legs. A crab's eyes stick out from its body on stalks.

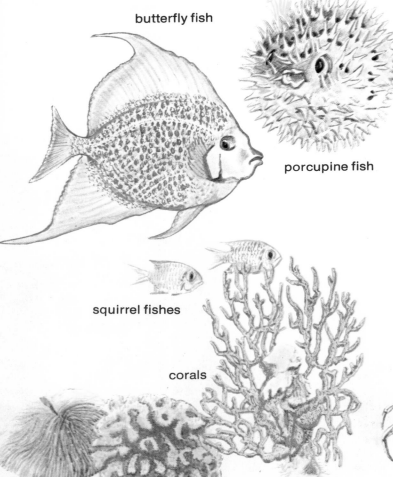

butterfly fish

porcupine fish

squirrel fishes

corals

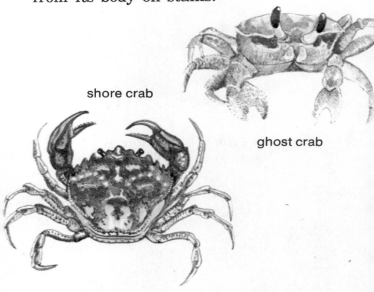

shore crab

ghost crab

crane

A large, long-legged bird that makes a loud trumpeting or whistling noise. Cranes communicate by doing a kind of dance. They bow, bob their heads and jump in the air.

cricket

A jumping insect with a chirping 'song'. The male cricket makes this noise by rubbing the left forewing against the right.

house cricket

crocodile

A large reptile found in lakes and rivers in hot climates. The crocodile and the alligator are almost identical. The main difference is that the fourth tooth on either side of the crocodile's lower jaw is very large, and can be seen when the crocodile's mouth is closed.

crocus

A flower belonging to the iris family. The wild crocus has white or violet flowers.

crow

A large black, or dark-coloured perching bird with a strong beak and bristly nostrils. The jay and the magpie belong to the crow family.

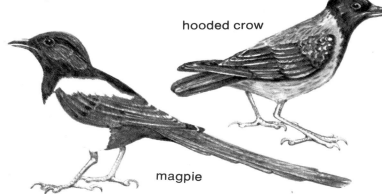

hooded crow

magpie

crustacean

An animal with a hard body-shell and two pairs of feelers. Most crustaceans live in water. Shrimps, crabs and lobsters are crustaceans.

cuckoo

A blue-grey bird with grey stripes on its white underparts. Its call sounds exactly like its name. The common cuckoo is well known for its habit of laying its eggs in other birds' nests.

common cuckoo

cypress

A coniferous tree with fern-like leaves, made up of many tiny needles.

Dd

daffodil

A plant with a single flower on each stem, usually white or yellow.

daisy

A small flower found in short grass. Its rounded leaves lie flat and close to the ground. The word daisy means 'day's eye' because the flower closes at night and in bad weather. Many different flowers belong to the daisy family.

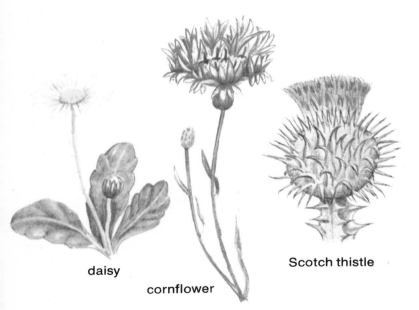

daisy

cornflower

Scotch thistle

deciduous

Without leaves for part of the year. Most deciduous trees have broad leaves, which lose water quickly. The leaves are dropped before winter so that the trees do not lose more water than they can take in.

deciduous forest

Forest found in temperate climates (those with warm summers and cool winters). Because broad leaves decay quickly and enrich the soil, there is usually much plant and animal life in deciduous forests.

serotine bat

tawny owl

jay

black woodpecker

orange-tip butterfly

mole

rabbit

earthstar fungus

dormouse

20

deer

A ruminant with bony antlers. Usually only male deer (stags) have antlers, but all reindeer and caribou have them.

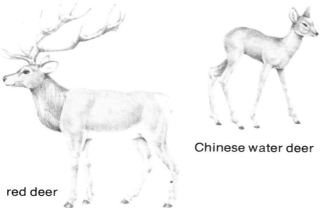

Chinese water deer

red deer

moose

elf owl

gila woodpecker

kangaroo rat

defence

Protection against enemies. Animals have many different ways of defending themselves. Bees, scorpions and wasps have stings. Tortoises and armadillos have armour. Hedgehogs and porcupines have quills. Many snakes have a venomous bite. The skunk has the most unusual defence of all—it makes a very nasty smell!

desert

A sandy or stony area with a very dry climate, usually very hot by day and very cold at night. Desert animals often hide from the heat in burrows or cracks. Some, like the kangaroo rat, spring along on their hindlegs, to avoid touching the hot ground. Cacti and other water-storing plants flourish in the desert.

The dry, windswept lands near the North Pole are sometimes called cold deserts. They do not have the same kind of plants and animals as other deserts (see **polar regions**).

kit fox

leopard tortoise

gila monster

cactus

scorpion

diurnal
Active during daylight.

divers
An order of large or medium-sized birds with stout bodies and short legs. They spend most of their time in water, and often move awkwardly on land.

red-throated diver

Cape hunting dog

Arctic loon

dog
A carnivorous mammal. Most wild dogs hunt in large groups, called packs. People have kept domestic dogs for thousands of years, both as workers and as pets.

German shepherd dog

collie

dingo

dolphin
A sea-living mammal belonging to the whale family. Dolphins are playful and highly intelligent. They communicate in a language of clicks and whistles.

dragonfly

A large, fast-flying insect, often very colourful. Dragonfly larvae hatch and live under water.

duck

A heavy-bodied, web-footed bird that lives on or near water.

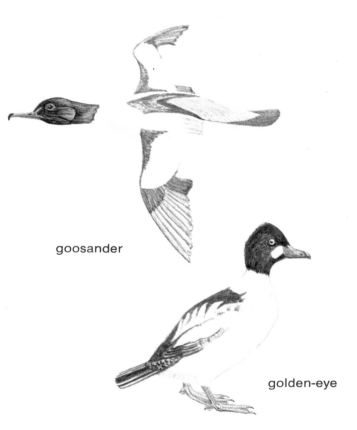

goosander

golden-eye

duck-billed platypus

A monotreme found in lakes and rivers in Australia. Its body is covered with fine fur and it has a short, fat tail, a duck-like beak and webbed feet for swimming.

Ee

eagle

A large bird of prey with a soaring flight. Some eagles are powerful enough to kill wolves and monkeys.

golden eagle

earwig

An insect with dangerous-looking 'tweezers' on its tail. It is harmless to humans. Unlike most other insects, earwigs look after their eggs and their babies.

echo-location

A system used by some animals to help them move around fast in poor light. The animals make sounds, and echoes bounce back from objects. The animals then avoid any nearby objects. Whales and dolphins, bats and cave-dwelling birds all use echo-location.

ecology

The study of environments and everything that lives in them.

eel

A fish with a snake-like body and a single long fin on its back. Eels are born in the Sargasso Sea and migrate across the Atlantic to the rivers of Europe and America. There they live and grow for five years or more, before returning to the Sargasso Sea to spawn and die.

egg

A cell that will grow into a baby animal. Some female animals keep the egg-cell inside them until the baby is complete. Others give birth to, or 'lay', the egg-cell with a shell round it. Inside the egg-cell is a store of food known as a yolk. The growing baby feeds on the yolk till it is hatched.

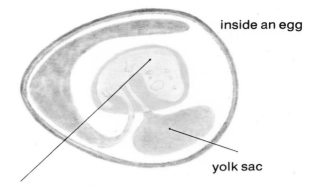

inside an egg

yolk sac

young animal or embryo

elephant

The largest and most powerful mammal on land weighing up to 6 tonnes. There are two species, African and Indian. The African elephant has larger ears and tusks.

African elephant

Indian elephant

elm

A tall tree with rough bark. It grows in fields and hedgerows rather than in woods. Dutch elm disease has killed thousands of trees in the past few years.

energy cycle

How the sun's energy, or light and heat, helps living things. Green plants use it to turn water and carbon dioxide into food (see **photosynthesis**). Then they return oxygen to the air. Animals breathe in the oxygen and eat the plants. Then they return waste matter to the soil and water and carbon dioxide to the air.

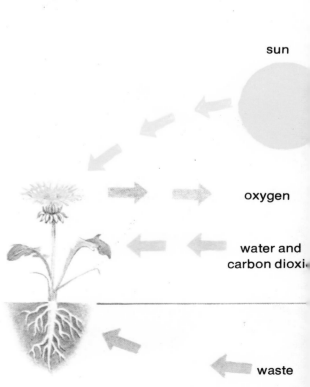

sun

oxygen

water and carbon dioxide

waste

environment

Where any plant or animal lives. Every living thing in an environment is part of the lives of all the others (see **food chain** and **balance of nature**).

eucalyptus

A very tall tree with strongly-scented leaves. It comes from Australia, where it is called the blue gum tree.

evergreen

In leaf all year round. Most conifers are evergreen, and so are some broad-leaved trees.

extinct

No longer in existence. Any species that once lived in the world but cannot be found today.

The dodo is an extinct bird

Ff

family

A number of species quite closely related to each other.

fern

A flowerless, spore-bearing green plant. Its leaves grow coiled up at first then slowly uncurl.

finch

A small perching bird that flies in flocks. All finches have stout bills for cracking seeds.

hawfinch   brambling

fish

A cold-blooded animal that lives, breathes and swims in water.

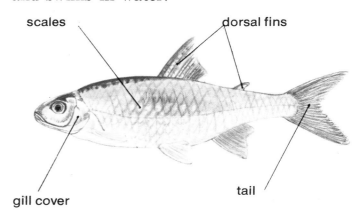

scales   dorsal fins

gill cover   tail

flamingo

A large, long-legged bird belonging to the order of striding birds. Its strange beak helps it filter its food from shallow water, and its pink colour comes from the shrimps and other small creatures it eats.

flightless birds

Birds that long ago stopped needing to fly. Their wings have become smaller or have almost disappeared. The penguin's wings have become flippers which help it to 'fly' through water. Some flightless birds, like the ostrich, can run so fast they have no need to fly. Others, like the kiwi, are nocturnal and hide in cracks or burrows during the day.

rhea

steamer duck

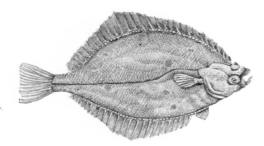

kiwi

flounder

A flat-fish that lives in the sea but migrates up rivers to feed.

fly

An insect with only one pair of wings (most other insects have two pairs).

flower

The part of many plants that makes the seeds to produce new plants. The male part of a flower, called the anther, produces pollen. The pistil, which is the female part, has a sticky bit called a stigma for catching pollen. To make new seeds, pollen has to be carried from an anther to a stigma. This can be done by wind, water or insects. Colourful flowers usually depend on insects to transmit pollen. They make nectar, which they keep deep inside their petals. Insects are attracted by the colour and enter the flower to drink the nectar. Pollen brushes off on them, and they then carry it to other flowers.

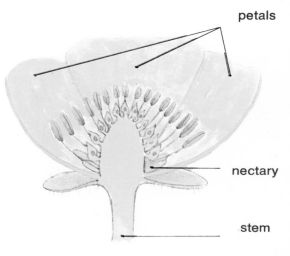
petals

nectary

stem

stigma

stamen

26

flying fish
A fish that can glide through the air. It has large fins that can be spread like wings.

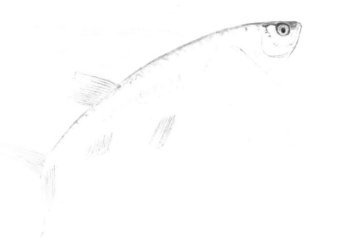

fossil
The remains of a plant or animal that was buried in prehistoric times. The thing itself, or the shape it left behind in sand or mud, has turned to stone over millions of years.

fox
A wild member of the dog family that hunts alone and by night.

food chain
How the plants and animals in a habitat need each other as sources of food.

owl

shrew

plant

bug

foxglove
A poisonous plant with a tall spike of drooping flowers. Each flower is shaped like a glove finger.

frog
A tailless amphibian with a smooth, moist skin, found in or near damp places. Its long hindlegs make it a powerful jumper, able to leap about six times its own length.

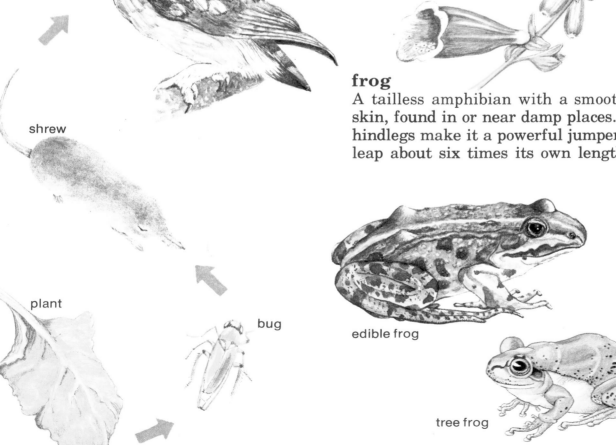

edible frog

tree frog

fruit

A case for the seeds of flowering plants. It can be hard or soft. A fruit with a single seed in it, like a cherry, is called a drupe. A berry like the raspberry is a cluster of drupes. Other berries, like the gooseberry, have many seeds inside a single fruit.

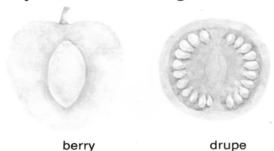

berry   drupe

fungus

A flowerless plant that produces spores instead of seeds. It has no green colouring and so cannot use the sunlight to make food. It lives on decaying things, or as a parasite.

parasol mushroom

cep

puff-ball

shaggy inkcap

chanterelle

fly agaric

Gg

gall

A growth on a plant, caused by a parasite. The oak apple is caused by the gall wasp, which lays its eggs in the bud of an oak tree. The larvae develop inside the bud, which grows into a gall instead of a leaf.

game birds

An order of heavy-bodied birds that scratch the ground for food. Some birds belonging to this order, like the pheasant and the partridge, are hunted by people for sport. Others, like the domestic hen and turkey, are farmed as food.

domestic hen

pheasant

geranium

One member of this varied family. Its long seed-pods look like birds' beaks.

gibbon

The smallest of the apes, and the one that looks least like human beings. It uses its extra-long arms to swing through trees.

giraffe

The tallest animal in the world—about three times the height of a man—with long legs and a very long neck. The giraffe roams the African grasslands in herds, using its very long tongue to gather leaves from the tree-tops as food. To reach the ground or to drink it has to splay its forelegs apart.

goat

A ruminant closely related to the sheep. Most goats have both horns and beards, though some domestic goats are hornless. Goats can cause a great deal of damage to their environment, as they will eat almost anything.

gorilla

The largest of the apes, and the one most closely related to human beings. It has a black skin and a powerful body covered with coarse black hair. Although just as intelligent as the chimpanzee, it is timid with people. Gorillas are found in Africa.

grass

A plant with tiny, petalless flowers.

grasshopper

A jumping insect related to the cricket. The male grasshopper 'sings' by rubbing its hindlegs against hard ridges on its wings.

grassland

An area that is not wet enough to be forest or dry enough to be desert. Warm grasslands, like the African savannah, have long grass and scattered trees. Where winters are cold, as on the North American prairie, the grass is shorter and trees are rare. Grasslands provide few hiding-places for predators or their prey. Most animals that live on them are sharp-sighted and fast-moving.

griffon vulture

African elephant

zebras

impala

lioness with cub

secretary bird

grass snake

A harmless snake that can be recognised by the pale collar on its neck. When attacked it either hisses or 'plays dead'.

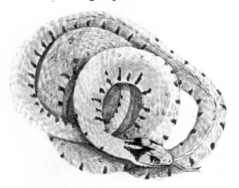

grooming

How animals keep clean. Some lick or bite their fur. Others roll in water, mud or dust. Sometimes one animal keeps another clean by feeding on its parasites. An African bird called the oxpecker lives on the ticks it picks off cattle.

gull

A wading bird with webbed feet and long, pointed wings. Gulls live on or near the sea, but some come inland to scavenge in towns or to follow the plough on farms.

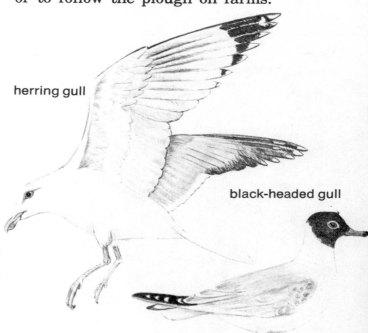

herring gull

black-headed gull

Hh

habitat
The particular part of an environment in which a plant or animal lives.

hamster
A short-tailed rodent with large cheek-pouches for carrying food.

hare
A fast-running furry mammal. It is related to the rabbit, but is larger and has longer ears and legs. Hares that live in cold climates grow a white coat in winter.

heather
A wiry evergreen plant with purple, bell-shaped flowers. The bilberry and the cranberry belong to the heather family, and both are good to eat.

bilberry   heather

hedgehog
A small, spiny insectivore. It rolls itself into a ball when frightened.

herbivore
An animal that eats only plants. Cattle, sheep, deer and horses are herbivores.

heron
A large bird with a long neck and legs, and a long, straight beak. Herons live near water and feed on fish and rodents. They belong to the order of striding birds.

heron

night heron

hibernation
Winter sleep. Many animals doze during winter, but some small creatures sleep very soundly. Their pulse slows down and they are cold to the touch. This is true hibernation. Small animals lose heat faster than large ones. They need to eat constantly, to give them enough energy to move around and keep warm. When they hibernate they use up very little energy. It is a way of staying alive when the weather is cold and food is scarce.

hippopotamus
A heavy mammal with leathery skin that lives in water during the hot African day. Its name means 'river horse'. In spite of its weight, the hippopotamus can run very fast. It attacks enemies with its huge, sharp, lower teeth.

home
A permanent shelter for an animal and its young. Animals often build their homes.

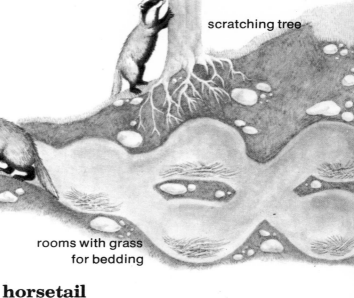

scratching tree

entrance

badger's set

rooms with grass for bedding

honeysuckle
A woody climbing plant with sweet-smelling flowers. The elder tree belongs to the honeysuckle family.

horsetail
A leafless, flowerless plant that produces spores instead of seeds. Exactly the same kind of plant grew in prehistoric times.

horse
A strong, fast-running mammal. People use horses for riding, racing and pulling heavy loads.

Percheron

human being
The most numerous, intelligent and widespread member of the primate order. Human beings always walk upright and they have a huge brain, longer legs than arms and very little hair. In all these ways they are different from their nearest relatives, the apes.

hyena
A short-tailed, dog-like mammal with powerful jaws, found in Africa and Asia. It kills live prey and also eats carrion.

horse chestnut
A tall tree with fan-shaped leaves. Inside its round, spiky green fruits are the polished nuts we call 'conkers'. When the leaves fall they leave scars shaped like horseshoes on the branches.

Ii

insect

An animal with three main parts to its body, and three pairs of legs. Most insects have a hard skeleton outside their body. Insects can be found in all parts of the world. There are about two hundred times as many named species of insects as there are mammals.

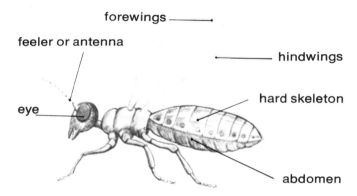

forewings

feeler or antenna

hindwings

eye

hard skeleton

abdomen

insect-eating plants

A number of plants use insects as part of their food. They use a sweet-smelling liquid to attract the insects. Then they trap them by closing on them or entangling them in sticky hairs.

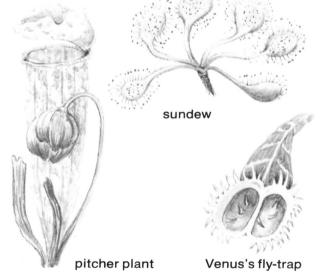

sundew

pitcher plant   Venus's fly-trap

insectivore

An animal that eats insects. There is an order of mammals called insectivores. They all have small eyes and ears, and whiskery snouts. Hedgehogs, moles and shrews belong to this order.

instinct

Knowing what to do without being taught. A bird is not taught to build a nest, nor a bee to gather pollen. They do these things by instinct.

invertebrate

An animal without a backbone. There are many invertebrates, including amoebae, worms, molluscs, crustaceans, insects and arachnids.

iris

A stout, hairless plant with narrow, sword-shaped leaves. The flag, the crocus and the gladiolus belong to the iris family.

ivy

A woody, evergreen climbing plant with clusters of tiny flowers. Ivy often twines itself round trees, but it is not a parasite.

Jj

jellyfish

A sea-living animal with a soft, jelly-like body. The jelly is mainly made up of water, so the animal dries up quickly if stranded on the beach. The jellyfish has stinging tentacles, or arms.

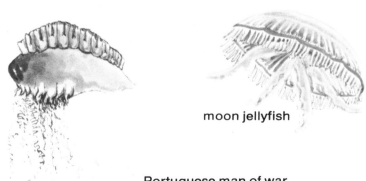

moon jellyfish

Portuguese man of war

jungle

Hot, wet forest found close to the Equator. There is no winter in the jungle, so there is food all year round for many different kinds of animals.

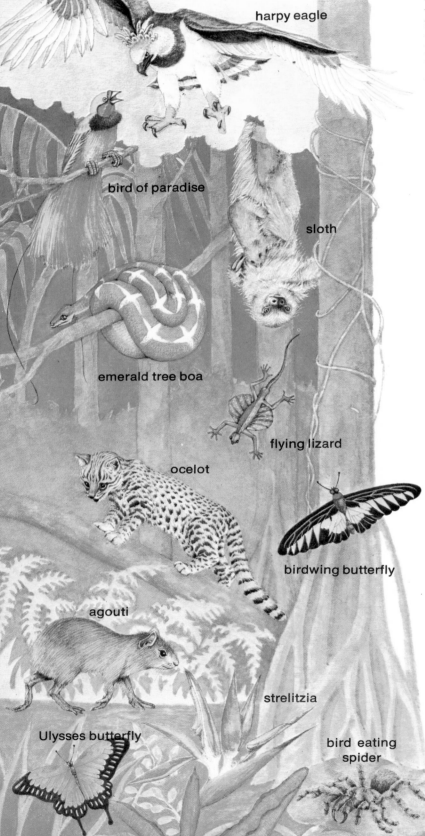

harpy eagle

bird of paradise

sloth

emerald tree boa

flying lizard

ocelot

birdwing butterfly

agouti

strelitzia

Ulysses butterfly

bird eating spider

Kk

kangaroo

A marsupial with strong hindlegs and a powerful tail, which help it to cover the ground in great bounds. The female has a pouch in which the babies live till they are fully developed. Kangaroos live in Australia.

kingfisher

A brilliantly coloured bird with a long, stout bill. It lives near fresh water and dives for fish. The Australian kookaburra belongs to the kingfisher family.

koala

An Australian marsupial that looks like a little bear. It lives in eucalyptus trees and eats their leaves. The koala has only one baby at a time. When the baby leaves its mother's pouch, it rides on her back.

Komodo dragon

The biggest living lizard, which grows to $3\frac{1}{2}$ m in length. It eats birds, mammals, other lizards and carrion.

Ll

ladybird

A small beetle that is very useful in gardens because it eats aphids. It is brightly coloured, with two, four, six or seven spots.

larva

A young animal, in the first stage of its life after hatching from an egg. A larva does not look or behave like the adults of its species. In order to become an adult, it must change its body structure completely (see **metamorphosis**).

lemur

A furry, long-tailed relative of the monkey. Lemurs are found only on the island of Madagascar and nearby. The largest is about the size of a cat, and the smallest is no bigger than a mouse.

leopard

A big cat found in Africa and Asia, in both hot and cold climates and in many different habitats, from jungle to snow-covered hills. Most leopards are spotted, but a few are black. The black ones, which may even be blue-eyed, are called panthers. Leopards are expert climbers, and often drop from trees on to their prey.

lichen

A spore-bearing plant with neither flowers nor roots. In fact it is two plants, because it is made up of a fungus and an alga living together. Lichen grows on the ground, on stone and on trees. It needs clean air to live and is never found where the air is badly polluted.

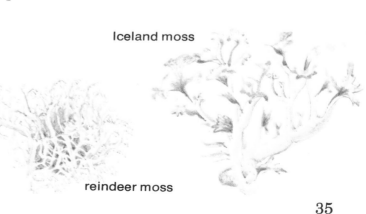

Iceland moss

reindeer moss

life cycle

The growth and development of any living thing, from the first to the last stage of its life.

purple emperor butterfly

chrysalis

egg

caterpillar

lily of the valley

A small plant with sweet-smelling, white, bell-like flowers. Many other plants belong to the lily family, including the hyacinth and the bluebell.

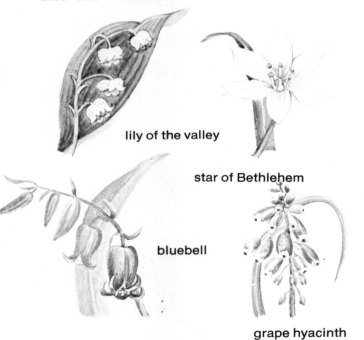

lily of the valley

star of Bethlehem

bluebell

grape hyacinth

lime

A tall tree with smooth, stringy bark and sweet-smelling blossom. Aphids love lime trees and their sticky honeydew often drips from the leaves.

lion

The second biggest member of the cat family. It is powerful and stockily built, and can kill prey with one blow of its paw. The male lion grows a mane of coarse hair around its head. Most of the hunting is done by the lioness. Lions live in groups called prides. They are found mostly in Africa, on open grasslands, although a few still live in India.

lizard

A reptile with clawed feet and a long tail. A very few, like the slow-worm, have no legs and look like snakes.

lobster

A large crustacean found in shallow parts of the sea. It uses its powerful claws to crush crabs and molluscs. Lobsters are blue with brown markings when alive, but turn red when cooked.

lyrebird

A shy perching bird found in Australia. The male displays his beautiful lyre-shaped tail in courtship. The lyrebird is a clever mimic, and can imitate other birds, barking dogs and various human noises.

Mm

magnolia
A broad-leaved tree with large, waxy flowers. These may be white, yellow, rose or purple.

mammal
A warm-blooded, vertebrate animal with hair on its body. All female mammals have milk to feed their young (see **monotreme**).

maple
A deciduous tree with ribbed bark and deeply-cut leaves. The sweet juice of the North American sugar maple is used to make syrup. The sycamore tree belongs to the maple family.

marmoset
A tiny monkey with a squeaky voice and claws on its feet. It is found in South America.

marsupial
A mammal whose babies are born very tiny and not fully developed. Most marsupials, like the kangaroo and the koala, have a pouch in which the helpless babies live and grow. A very few species, such as some American opossums, have no pouch and the babies cling to the mother's body. Marsupials are found only in Australia and America.

mating
The coming together of two animals for the purpose of breeding young. When animals live together in herds or colonies, one male often has a group of females with which he mates. The group is known as a harem and the male will fight for his possession of it. The sea-lion and the red deer mate in this way. Other animals mate with any member of the opposite sex, but birds have only one mate at a time during each breeding season. Some animals mate for life and stay together to bring up their families. The jackdaw, the badger, the swan and the wolf all mate in this way.

mayfly
An insect whose larvae live under water. Adult mayflies have no mouth. They only live long enough to mate and lay eggs.

metamorphosis
A complete change in both body structure and habits. For example, a butterfly begins life as a larva, or caterpillar. Then it changes to a pupa, or chrysalis. Inside the skin of the chrysalis, the caterpillar breaks up and re-forms into a butterfly. The skin splits and the butterfly struggles out. Many other insects become adult by metamorphosis, as do starfishes, frogs and toads.

migration

Regular journeys made by a species of animal from one part of the world to another and back again. Insect-eating birds, like the swallow and the cuckoo, leave northern lands in autumn and fly south to find a more plentiful food supply. In spring they return north to breed. Many other animals, including the eel and the salmon also migrate. The reasons for migration are often puzzling, and so is the ability of animals to find their way over vast distances. We now know that birds have a built-in 'compass' and that both birds and insects can tell the time of day by the position of the sun. It seems likely that these abilities, plus instinct, sight, memory and even smell, help migrating animals to make their astonishing journeys.

millipede

A slow-moving animal whose name means 'a thousand feet'. Millipedes do have a great many legs, but not as many as a thousand.

mistletoe

An evergreen plant that lives on the branches of trees. It is a semi-parasite because it lives partly on the juices of trees and partly on air.

mole

A small insectivore with tiny eyes and velvety fur. It has large forelimbs for digging.

star-nosed mole

mollusc

A soft-bodied invertebrate. Snails, squid and octopuses are all molluscs.

mongoose

A slender, furry mammal that kills snakes and eats eggs.

monkey

A mammal belonging to the primate order and related to lemurs, apes and humans. Monkeys have expressive faces and human-looking hands. Most monkeys also have a tail.

monotreme

A mammal that lays eggs, but also has milk for its young. There are only two kinds of monotreme, the duck-billed platypus and the echidna, and both are found in Australia.

moose

A very large deer that lives in cold climates. It is also known as the elk.

mosquito

A 'biting' fly. The male feeds on nectar, but the female feeds on the blood of mammals. She has a needle-like mouth for puncturing skin.

moss

A small, green, flowerless plant which bears spores. It grows on soil, rocks, walls and tree trunks.

moth

An insect related to the butterfly. A moth's feelers are feathery, while a butterfly's have a knob on the end. Most moths fly by night.

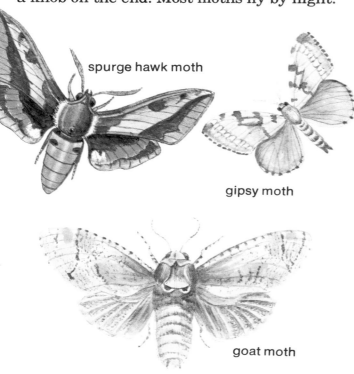

spurge hawk moth

gipsy moth

goat moth

mouse

A small nocturnal rodent with bright, beady eyes, large rounded ears and a long tail.

mulberry

A short, squat tree with heart-shaped leaves. The berries of the black mulberry make good jam. Silkworms feed on the leaves of the white mulberry.

Nn

nectar

A sweet juice produced by many flowering plants.

nest

A shelter built or found by an animal, to use mainly while rearing its young.

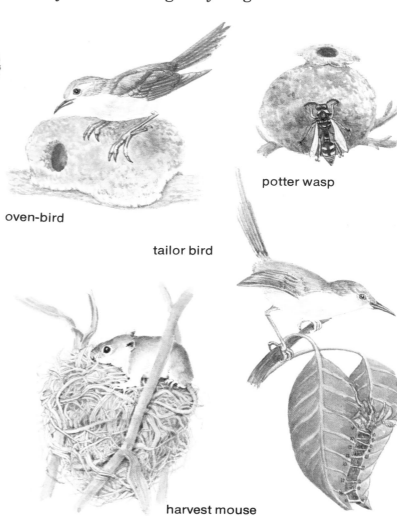

oven-bird

potter wasp

tailor bird

harvest mouse

newt

An amphibian with a tail which it uses for swimming. It has a smooth skin, which sometimes has lumps or warts on it. The male newt often grows a crest along his back.

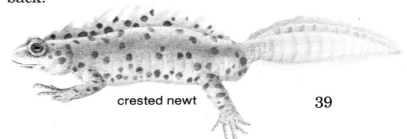

crested newt

nightjar

A nocturnal bird that flies with a gaping beak to catch insects. One species of nightjar, the poorwill, is the only bird known to hibernate.

nightjar

poorwill

nocturnal

Active during the night.

Like many nocturnal animals, the tarsier has huge eyes

nut

A large, hard seed produced by a tree or shrub. The hazel nut, the brazil nut and the walnut are all the seeds of trees.

walnut

hazel nut

Brazil nut

Oo

oak

A tall, broad-leaved tree with strong, heavy wood. It can live for more than a thousand years. The hard fruit of the oak is called the acorn.

acorn

octopus

A sea-living mollusc with eight arms, or tentacles. It has a large brain and good eyesight. When alarmed it changes colour, and releases an inky liquid called sepia.

olive

A tree with narrow silvery-green leaves. It is known for its fruit and the oil that is pressed out of it. The ash tree belongs to the olive tree family.

omnivore

An animal that eats both plant and animal food. Most animals are basically either carnivores or herbivores, but many will eat both kinds of food. Bears, badgers, crows and human beings are all omnivorous.

opossum

A marsupial found only in America. It is nocturnal and lives in trees, feeding mainly on insects, frogs and birds. Most species of opossum have pouches for their young, but a few do not.

orang-utan

A large ape found in the jungles of Malaysia and Borneo. Its name means 'old man of the woods'. The male orang-utan grows a large pouch of skin round his face.

orchid

A plant with long, smooth leaves and oddly-shaped flowers. The flowers are often spotted or brilliantly coloured.

order

The word used to describe a number of animal families that are related to each other. For example, the lion belongs to the cat family and the wolf belongs to the dog family. The cat family and the dog family both belong to the order of carnivores, so the lion and the wolf belong to the same order.

ornithology

The study of birds.

ostrich

The largest living bird, found on open grasslands in Africa. It is flightless, but can run very fast with its long, powerful legs and strong, two-toed feet.

owl

A nocturnal bird that preys on all kinds of smaller animals. It has a hooked beak and a large head with the eyes at the front. An owl can turn its head in a full circle, or even upside down.

tawny owl

eagle owl

oyster

A bivalve found in the sea. If a grain of sand gets inside an oyster shell, the oyster covers it with a smooth, shiny substance to stop it scratching. This is how pearls are made.

Pp

palm
A tree whose leaves grow directly from the top of its trunk. Dates and coconuts are produced by different species of palm trees.

panda
A mammal found on mountains in China. There are two species. The giant panda looks like a black and white bear and the red panda looks more like a fox. Both feed on bamboo shoots.

giant panda

red panda

parasite
A plant or animal that lives in, or on, another species. A parasite takes food but gives nothing in return.

parrot
A bird with a heavy, hooked beak, found only in warm climates. It is an excellent mimic of human speech and other sounds. The macaw and the cockatoo belong to the parrot family.

macaw

African grey parrot

peacock
A bird that belongs to the order of game birds, though it is now neither hunted nor eaten. The male bird, or peacock (the female is called the peahen) has a long, trailing tail. When lifted up, this makes a brilliant display with a pattern of 'eyes'.

pelican
A large, web-footed water bird. It has a huge pouch under its beak which it uses like a net for catching fish.

penguin

A flightless swimming and diving bird with flippers instead of wings. It has an upright body with a white front and a black back. Penguins are found only in the very cold areas close to the South Pole.

emperor penguin

macaroni penguin

perch

A freshwater fish with spiny fins and sharp-edged scales.

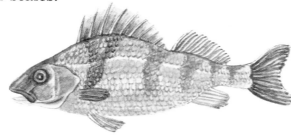

perching birds

An order of birds with feet suited only to perching and walking. They never have webbed feet, even if they feed in or near water. All the well known songbirds, such as the thrush, the blackbird, the robin and the lark are perching birds.

satin bowerbird

house sparrow

photosynthesis

How green plants use sunlight. All green plants contain a substance called chlorophyll, which gives them their colour. Chlorophyll traps sunlight, and uses it to turn water and carbon dioxide from the air into glucose. Glucose, along with minerals drawn from the soil, provides plants with food to live and grow.

pig

A short-legged, stoutly built mammal with a long, blunt snout. The domestic pig is descended from the ferocious wild boar, and is farmed as food. Its skin is cured for leather.

wild boar

pigeon

A plump bird with a small head, a short bill and a cooing voice. Pigeons are scavengers in many towns and cities.

pike

A freshwater fish with a large jaw and many sharp teeth.

pine

A coniferous tree that carries its needles in clumps of two, three or five. Its wood is used for furniture and paper-making.

plane

A broad-leaved tree that sheds its bark in patches as it grows older. This gives its trunk a dappled look.

plankton

Tiny living things that drift in water. Some are algae and others animals. They are an important food for some sea animals such as the blue whale.

plant

A living thing that feeds by means of its leaves, stems or roots (see **energy cycle**). A plant cannot move around of its own accord.

polar regions

The very cold areas around the North Pole (the Arctic) and the South Pole (the Antarctic). Polar regions have no sun for half the year, and much of the land and sea is always frozen. A few plants and animals live on the land, but the seas are rich in plankton and can support much more life.

pollen

A fine dust produced by flowers. Each grain contains the male cell needed to fertilise a female cell, that is, to enable it to produce the seed of a new plant.

pollution

The poisoning of air, land and water with waste material and chemicals (see **conservation**).

ponds and lakes

Areas of fresh water with little or no movement of water in and out.

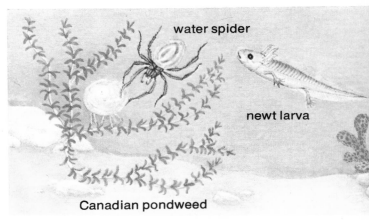

water spider

newt larva

Canadian pondweed

poppy

A plant with a single large flower at the end of each hairy stem. Wild poppies have four floppy petals.

common red poppy

yellow horned poppy

rockhopper penguin

adelie penguins

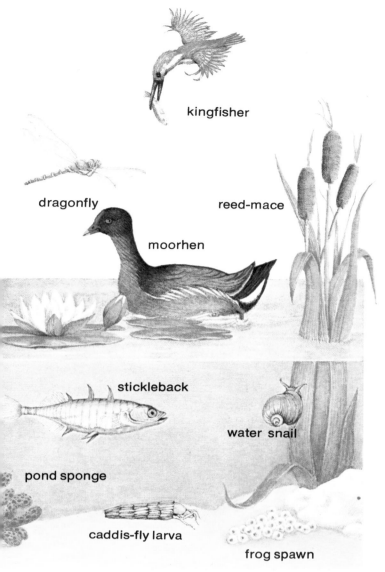

kingfisher

dragonfly

reed-mace

moorhen

stickleback

water snail

pond sponge

caddis-fly larva

frog spawn

predator
An animal that kills other animals for food.

preening
How a bird uses its beak to groom itself after a bath. First it rubs its feathers to dry them. Then it spreads them with oil taken from a gland at the base of its tail. The oil keeps the feathers waterproof.

prehistoric
Belonging to the time before written history. Fossils show us the plants and animals that lived millions of years ago. Almost all are now extinct, but a few can still be found.

prey
Any animal killed by another for food.

porcupine
A large rodent with sharp, spiny quills. There are two families of porcupines. One is found in Africa and Asia and the other in America. American porcupines live mainly in trees, while the others live on the ground.

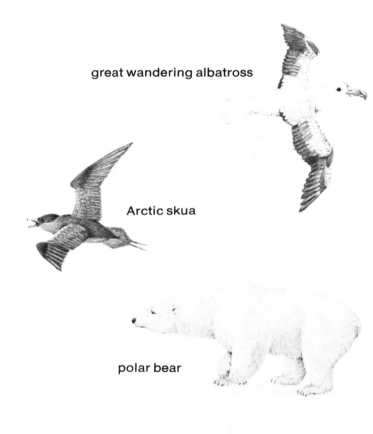

great wandering albatross

Arctic skua

polar bear

ground porcupine

grey seals

Arctic fox

ptarmigan

lemmings

45

primate

The order of mammals to which lemurs, bush-babies, monkeys, apes and humans belong.

proboscis monkey

A leaf-eating monkey found in Borneo. It gets its name from its strange long nose.

puma

A big cat found all over America, from icy mountain slopes to hot jungles. It varies in colour from yellow-brown to reddish. The puma is an excellent climber and can spring easily from tree to tree.

pupa

A stage in the life cycle of some insects. It comes between the larva and the adult.

python

A snake related to the boa, which also kills its prey by squeezing it. Most pythons are boldly patterned in browns and yellows.

Qq

quetzal

A shimmering green Central American bird, with very long tail feathers and a red breast.

Rr

rabbit

A furry mammal related to the hare. It has long ears and a short tail with a white underside. Rabbits live together in large groups, in underground warrens which they dig out with their feet.

raccoon

A short-legged, roly-poly mammal found in America. It has a black 'mask' across its face and black bands on its tail. The raccoon fishes in shallow pools with its forepaws, searching for frogs, crustaceans and fishes to eat. It is omnivorous, and is often a scavenger in towns.

rat

A nocturnal rodent related to the mouse. It has a furry body and a long, hairless tail. Rats will eat anything, from fruit and seeds to plaster and even soap.

rattlesnake

A venomous snake found in America. The rattle on the end of its tail is made of a material rather like our fingernails. It is made in sections that fit into each other loosely, so that when it is shaken the sections click together. Shaken fast, it sounds like a hissing kettle. No one knows why the rattlesnake rattles. It may be a warning to other animals to keep away. For example, a weasel will attack a rattlesnake only if the rattle has been removed.

ray

A sea fish with a very flat body. It swims by flapping its wing-like fins.

regeneration

The growing of new body parts to replace lost ones. Some lizards, when caught by the end of the tail, can snap it off and escape. Later they grow a new tail tip. Newts can do the same, and crabs can re-grow legs or claws. Starfishes can re-grow a broken-off arm. Even odder, the broken-off arm can grow into a new starfish.

reptile

A cold-blooded animal with a rough or scaly skin. Crocodiles, lizards, snakes and tortoises are reptiles.

rhinoceros

A strong, heavy mammal with a thick, leathery skin. It has a horn, or horns, rising up from its snout. These horns are not made of bone, but of a tightly-packed mass of hard fibres. Rhinos live in Asia and Africa.

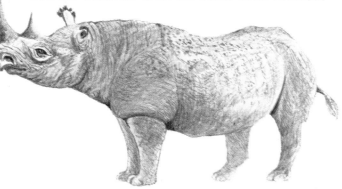

rivers and streams

Fresh, flowing water. Mountain streams flow too fast for most plants to take root, and few animals live in them. Wider, slower rivers have much more life in and around them.

rodent

A furry mammal with large, curved front teeth. These teeth never stop growing, so rodents have to gnaw all the time to keep them short. Rodents are found in all parts of the world except the Antarctic.

root

The part of a plant that anchors it in the ground and carries water and food to the stem.

rose

A deciduous shrub with spiny thorns on its stems and glossy fruits known as hips. Its flowers are often sweet-smelling. The strawberry, the raspberry, the bramble and the hawthorn all belong to the rose family.

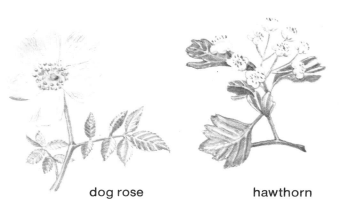

dog rose   hawthorn

ruminant

An animal with three or four compartments in its stomach. It swallows as much food as it can at a time. Later it brings a ball of food back from its stomach to its mouth, to chew at leisure. Deer and cattle are ruminants.

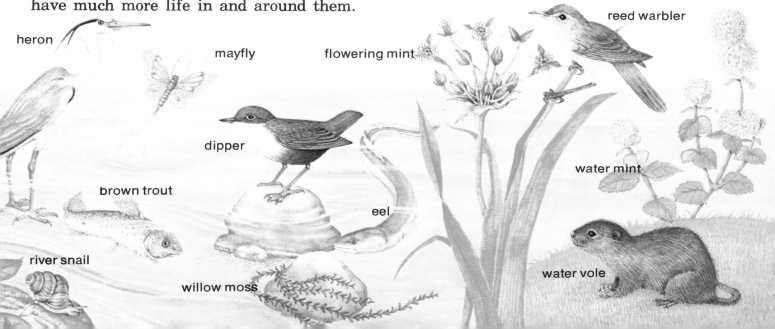

heron

mayfly

flowering mint

reed warbler

dipper

brown trout

eel

water mint

river snail

water vole

willow moss

Ss

salmon

A fast-swimming, predatory fish. Salmon are born in rivers and live there for about two years. Then they swim to the sea, where they live for several more years until they are ready to mate. By then they may be a very long way from the river where they were born. Somehow—no one really knows how—they find their way back to it and travel up river, leaping any obstacles in their path, till they find a suitable spot to spawn.

sandpiper

A wading bird with a piping call found near fresh water or by the sea. It uses its long beak to probe in mud or sand for food.

dunlin

sandpiper

ruff

some birds belonging to the sandpiper family

scavenger

An animal that does a useful clearing-up job. A scavenger feeds on dead plants, carrion, waste and rubbish. Vultures, hyenas and scarab beetles are scavengers. Foxes and coyotes living near towns often scavenge in rubbish bins.

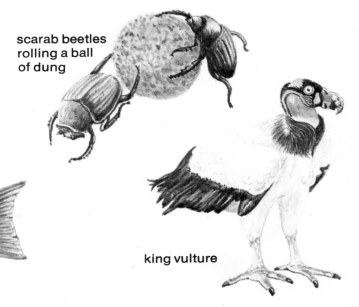

scarab beetles rolling a ball of dung

king vulture

scorpion

An arachnid found only in warm climates. It has a poisonous sting in its tail. Scorpions do not lay eggs, but give birth to live young.

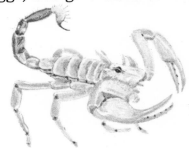

sea

The salt water that covers nearly three-quarters of the Earth's surface. All rivers pick up salts from the soil as they travel over it. At the end of their journey their water pours into the sea. When the heat of the sun evaporates sea water (turns it into gas) the salt in it is left behind. Seas in hot climates evaporate more than those in cold climates, and are therefore saltier. The different layers of the sea, from the sunny surface to the lightless depths, provide habitats for a huge variety of creatures. (See **tide**.)

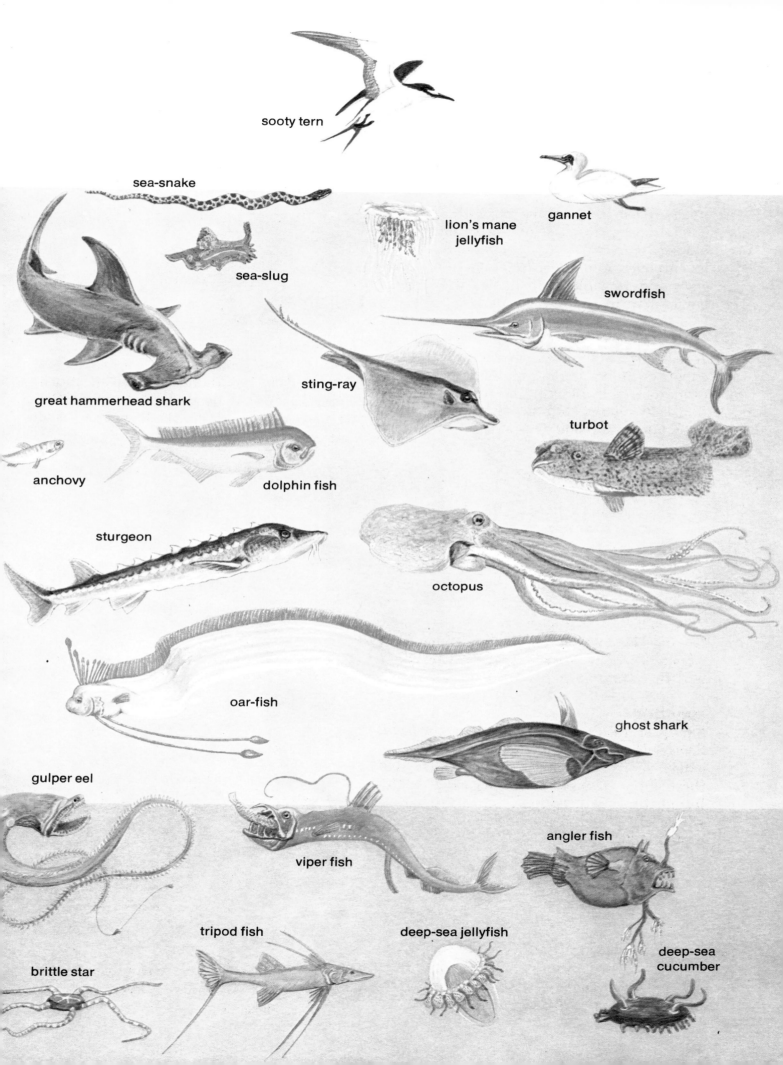

sooty tern

sea-snake

lion's mane
jellyfish

gannet

sea-slug

swordfish

great hammerhead shark

sting-ray

turbot

anchovy

dolphin fish

sturgeon

octopus

oar-fish

ghost shark

gulper eel

angler fish

viper fish

brittle star

tripod fish

deep-sea jellyfish

deep-sea
cucumber

sea-anemone

A sea animal that lives attached to a rock. It has a mouth at its centre, with tentacles, or arms, arranged around it. It catches live prey with its tentacles.

sea-horse

A small fish that swims upright. It has a horse-like head and a long tail that can be twined round seaweeds. The male sea-horse has a pouch into which the female lays her eggs and in which the babies grow. Seahorses live in shallow warm seas.

seal

A sea-living mammal with sleek fur. It is an expert swimmer but moves clumsily on land, dragging itself along by its fore flippers. A seal's ears do not show because they have no flaps on the outside.

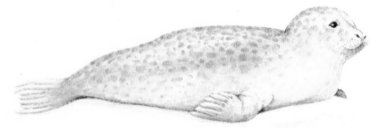

sea-lion

A large, heavy seal with ear flaps that show. During the mating season the males fight savagely for the possession of their territory and their harem of females.

seashore

Sandy or rocky areas washed by the tide. Seaweeds cannot anchor themselves to sandy shores, and most animals that live there bury themselves in the sand. Many living things can be found on rocky shores where the seaweed provides both food and protection.

sea-urchin

A sea animal with a hard outside skeleton, or shell. It is rounded in shape and covered with sharp spines. Sea-urchins live mainly in shallow water near rocky shores, and in coral reefs. Some live in holes they bore in rocks by using their spines and teeth.

seaweed

An alga that grows in the sea or on rocky shores. It is not found in deep or murky water because it needs light to grow. Seaweeds are valuable as fertiliser, and some can also be cooked and eaten.

bladder wrack

sea lettuce

coral weed

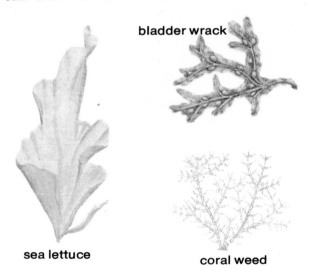

mussels

oyster-catcher

skate's egg case

spiny spider crab

sea-anemone

sea-cucumber

barnacles

prawn

blenny

dulse

hermit crab

seed

The part of a plant that will grow into a new plant. A seed must travel away from its parent plant to root in fresh ground.

how seeds travel

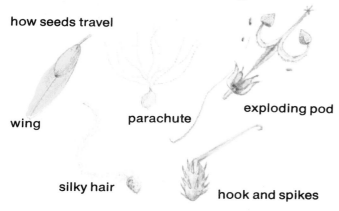

wing

parachute

exploding pod

silky hair

hook and spikes

sequoia

An enormous coniferous tree, also known as the redwood. The most massive tree in the world is a giant sequoia growing in California. It stands 83 m tall.

shark

A cigar-shaped fish with rough scales and a triangular fin on its back (the dorsal fin). The shark is a scavenger and will eat almost anything including tins, boxes and bottles. The great white shark is the most dangerous to humans because it is so large and aggressive. Some species of sharks lay eggs, while others give birth to live young.

great white shark

sheep

A ruminant related to cattle and goats. Wild sheep are still found in mountainous areas in various parts of the world. Domestic sheep have much thicker, heavier coats than wild sheep. They are farmed for their wool and their meat.

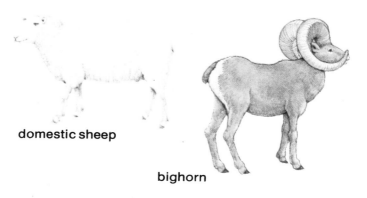

domestic sheep

bighorn

shell

A protective covering. The shells we find on the seashore are the hard outside skeletons of molluscs.

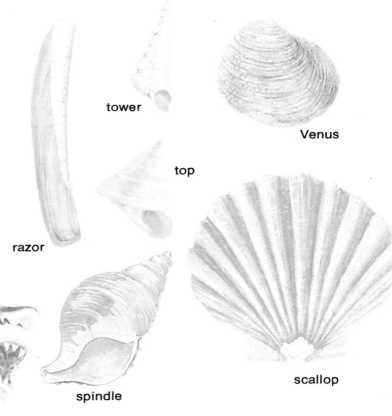

tower

Venus

top

razor

spindle

scallop

shrew

A tiny, furry insectivore with a long pointed nose and a long tail. Many shrews live for only one year.

shrub

A woody plant. A shrub has many branches, but no main trunk.

dogwood

silkworm

Not a worm, but the caterpillar stage of a moth. It spins a fine thread to make its cocoon. When the cocoon is unwound, the thread is used to weave silk cloth. The silkworm eats only the leaves of the white mulberry tree.

skunk

A mammal belonging to the weasel family. It is about the size of a small cat, and has a long coat patterned or striped in black and white. Skunks defend themselves by spraying a foul-smelling liquid on their attackers.

sloth

A mammal found in the jungles of South America. It cannot walk or stand on the ground, but can only move along branches while hanging upside down. Sloths move very, very slowly and often sleep for eighteen hours a day.

snail

A mollusc that carries its 'home'—a whorled shell—on its back. It lays a trail of silvery slime as it moves, to help it on its way. A snail has two pairs of tentacles, like little horns, on its head. It carries its eyes on the tips of the longer pair. Water snails are slightly different from land snails. They lay no slime and have only one pair of tentacles, with the eyes at the base.

snake

A legless reptile that swallows its prey whole. Some snakes are venomous.

social insects

Insects that live and work together in groups called colonies. In every nest or hive there is a *queen*, whose job is to lay eggs. The male insects, or *drones,* mate with the queen so that she can lay eggs. There are also *workers* who may be males or females, but who do not mate and cannot lay eggs. The job of the workers is to gather food and look after the nest and the larvae. Some ants and termites have special, larger workers called *soldiers* to defend the nest. All ants are social insects. So are termites, honey-bees, bumble-bees and some kinds of wasps.

entrance

egg hatchery

worker with food

larvae

queen laying

larvae become
cocoons and then ants

spawn

The mass of eggs laid in water by fishes, amphibians and some molluscs and crustaceans. When these animals lay their eggs, we say they are spawning.

species

A particular kind of plant or animal. Members of any species mate only with each other. They do not mate with members of another species, even though they may be related. For example, the thrush and the blackbird belong to different species within the same family and do not mate with each other.

spider

An arachnid that eats insects. Most spiders spin silken webs to trap their prey.

spider monkey

A slender monkey with long, spidery arms and legs. It lives high in the tree-tops of South American jungles, and uses its long tail to hang from branches while it picks fruit to eat.

sponge

An animal found in seas, lakes and rivers. It feeds by filtering tiny plants and animals from the water. The bath sponge is fished in warm seas and left to dry in the sun. The part we use is actually the soft skeleton of the animal.

bath sponge

spore

A tiny cell produced by many flowerless plants. Each spore released by a plant grows into a container for male sperm cells and female egg cells. When an egg cell has been fertilised by a sperm cell, it produces a new plant.

spruce

A tall, cone-shaped coniferous tree. Its white wood is often used for making paper. Young spruces are used as Christmas trees.

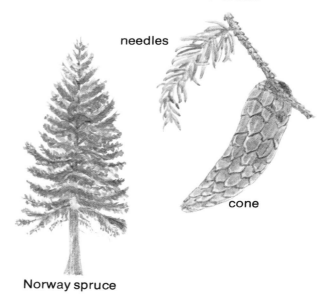

needles

cone

Norway spruce

squid

A sea-living mollusc with ten arms, or tentacles. It is a powerful swimmer and can actually 'jet propel' itself. It does this by shooting out a blast of water through a kind of funnel in its body.

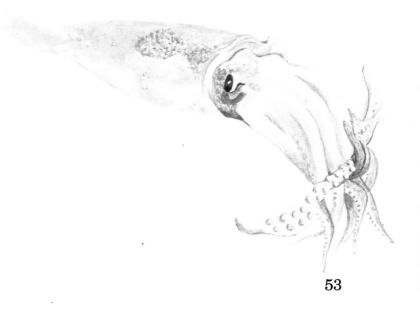

squirrel

A furry rodent with large, bright eyes. Some squirrels, like the chipmunk and the gopher, live on the ground. Others, like the red squirrel and the grey squirrel, live in trees where they build a permanent home called a drey. Tree squirrels have long bushy tails. Flying squirrels are tree squirrels that live in Asia and America. They have a flap of fur-covered skin and muscle on each side of their body, stretching from wrist to ankle. By spreading this they can glide from one tree to another.

red squirrel

starfish

A rough-skinned sea animal, related to the sea-urchin and star-like in shape. Most species have five arms, but species with as many as fifty arms have been found.

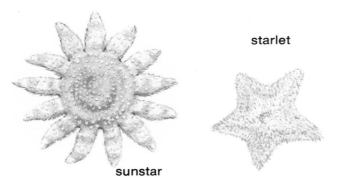
sunstar

starlet

sting

A part of a plant or animal used to transmit poison.

stoat

A small carnivore with a long, slender body. Its coat is red-brown on top and white underneath, and it has a black tip to its tail. In cold climates the stoat grows a white winter coat as camouflage in the snow.

54

striding birds

An order of birds with long necks and long legs. They have long, hard beaks and short webbing between their toes. Storks and herons belong to this order.

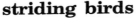

scarlet ibis

roseate spoonbill

white stork

sturgeon

A large fish with bony plates instead of scales. It migrates to rivers to spawn, then returns to the sea. When a female sturgeon is caught the eggs, called the roe, are removed. They are good to eat, and are known as caviar.

swallow

A small perching bird with a short, flat beak and a wide mouth for catching insects while it is flying. It has long wings and a long, forked tail. (See **migration**.)

house-martin

swallow

swan

A large, long-necked water-living bird. Most species are white, but the Australian swan is black. Because they are so large and heavy, swans often have some trouble getting into the air, but once there they fly powerfully and gracefully.

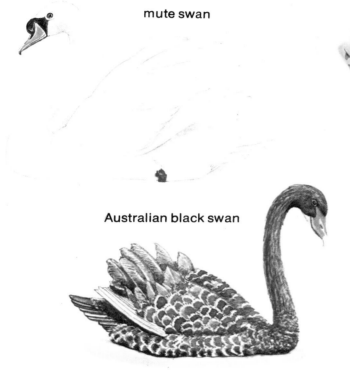

mute swan

Australian black swan

swift

A fast-flying bird with long, narrow wings, which catches insects in flight. It has weak legs and tiny feet, and seldom lands on the ground. Like many insect-eating birds, it migrates to a warm climate before winter. The swift is not related to the swallow, but belongs to the same order as the tiny nectar-drinking humming-bird of America.

humming-bird

swift

Tt

tadpole

The larva of a frog or a toad.

the life cycle of the frog

termite

A social insect that feeds mainly on wood. Some termites build enormous nests, as big as a house. Queen termites live for fifty years or more—far longer than any other insect.

territory

An area defended by an animal against others of the same species. Territory may be needed for feeding or mating or nesting, or for all of these activities.

thrush

A perching bird with a brown back and dark spots on its pale breast. It is best known for its sweet, loud, clear song. The blackbird belongs to the thrush family.

blackbird

song thrush

tide

The rise and fall of the sea, caused by the gravitational 'pull' of the Moon and the Sun on the Earth's surface.

tiger

The largest of the big cats, which may reach well over 3 m in length, found in Asia. Its reddish-fawn coat, striped with black, provides good camouflage among trees and long grass. Tigers hunt alone or in pairs. They dislike great heat, and often lie in water to keep cool.

tit

A small, sturdy bird with a short beak. Tits usually eat insects, but in winter they will eat seeds. They are active little birds that hop around quickly and often hang upside down.

blue tit   coal tit

toad

An amphibian very like a frog, but with shorter hindlegs and a drier, warty skin. It usually moves by crawling. Toads spend the day in holes in walls or under tree roots. At dusk they come out to feed on worms, snails and insects. During winter they hibernate.

common toad

tortoise

A reptile that lives inside a bony shell. It has no teeth and tears its food apart with its horny bill. Tortoises have been known to live for well over a hundred years. They hibernate in cold climates.

Greek tortoise

tracks

Footprints of animals which show up in mud, sand, dust or snow.

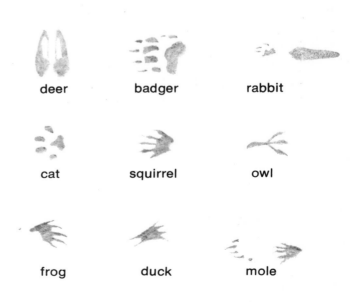

deer   badger   rabbit

cat   squirrel   owl

frog   duck   mole

tree

A plant whose dense, closely-packed cells form the hard substance known as wood. The wooden stem of a tree is called the trunk. Food is stored in it, and water travels upwards through it from the roots to the leaves. Because wood is so strong, trees can grow bigger and taller than any other plants.

turkey

A large, heavy bird with naked red and blue skin on its head and neck. The male turkey makes a gobbling noise. The turkey belongs to the order of game birds, and is eaten on Christmas Day in many parts of the world, and on Thanksgiving Day in the United States.

turtle

A water-living reptile that lives inside a bony shell. It is related to the tortoise. Freshwater turtles are called terrapins or pond tortoises. They have flattened shells and webbed toes. Turtles that live in the sea have flippers.

hawk's-bill turtle

Blanding's terrapin

Uu

umbellifer

A plant with hollow stems and flowers arranged on 'spokes' like an umbrella. The flowers are tiny and clustered together to form a canopy. They may be white, pink or yellow.

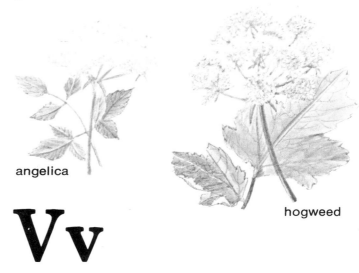

angelica

hogweed

Vv

vampire

A bat that drinks the blood of larger mammals and birds. It is the only mammal that is a parasite. Vampires are quite small and do not drink much blood, but they are dangerous because they spread disease.

venom

Poison used by some plants and animals to kill or paralyse their prey. Others use it to defend themselves. When a snake bites its prey the venom is injected through hollow teeth called fangs.

vertebrate

An animal with a backbone.

violet

A plant with heart-shaped leaves and a single flower on each stalk. The pansy belongs to the violet family.

violet   pansy

viper

A venomous snake that preys on frogs, toads and lizards. Most vipers have zigzag or diamond-shaped markings.

vole

A small rodent with a short tail and a blunt snout. Voles are found everywhere north of the Equator. The water vole, sometimes called the 'water rat', and the American musk-rat, which is trapped for its long fur, are the largest members of the vole family.

vulture

A large bird of prey that feeds on carrion. It is the only bird of prey with naked skin on its head and neck.

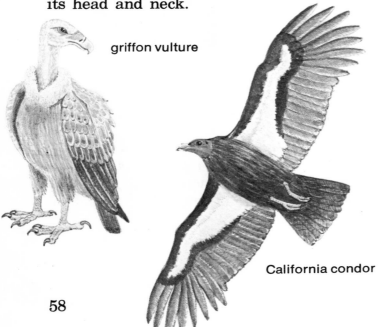

griffon vulture

California condor

Ww

wading birds

An order of birds that live on or near water or in damp meadows. They have long toes to help them walk on soft sand or mud, and some have webbed feet. Their beaks can be strong for dealing with fish or crustaceans, or long and slender for probing sand or mud. Gulls, puffins, plovers, sandpipers and oyster-catchers belong to this order.

American jacana

avocet

walrus

A heavy mammal with flippers, related to the seal and the sea-lion. The walrus has a rough, wrinkled, almost hairless skin and both males and females have long, thick tusks. Walruses are found mainly in shallow coastal water around the North Pole.

warm-blooded animal

An animal that can keep its body at an even temperature, whether its surroundings are hot or cold. Doing this uses up a lot of energy. Cold-blooded animals can go without food for quite long spells, but warm-blooded animals must eat regularly to keep up their energy supply. Birds and mammals are warm-blooded.

warthog

A member of the pig family found on grasslands all over Africa. It gets its name from the warty lumps on its face. The warthog has curving tusks, a tough skin and a mane of coarse hair on its neck.

wasp

A black-and-yellow striped insect with a sting on the end of its body. It is related to bees and ants. Most wasps are solitary, but a few live in colonies (see **social insects**).

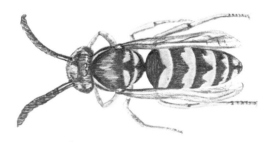

water cycle

The Sun's heat evaporates water (changes it to gas) and makes it rise into the air. When the water cools, or condenses, it falls back to Earth as rain or snow.

water-lily

A plant that grows from the bed of ponds, lakes or slow-flowing rivers. The leaves and the white or yellow flowers float on the surface of the water.

weasel

The smallest carnivore in the world, about 28 cm long, including tail. It is related to the stoat and looks similar, but is smaller and has no black tip to its tail. The weasel eats rats and mice, and will also attack rabbits and birds.

whale

A mammal that looks like a fish, but is warm-blooded and has to rise to the surface of the sea to breathe air. Before taking a breath the whale blows out used air through the nostril, or blow-hole, on top of its head. Some whales have teeth and feed on fish. Others have a 'comb' of bony plates called baleen. Through this they filter plankton from the water.

killer whale

willow

A deciduous tree or shrub usually found near water. It bears its flowers in catkins. One of the largest and most beautiful willows is the weeping willow, whose branches droop almost to the ground.

witches' broom

A thick clump of small twigs growing on the branch of a tree. Attack by an insect or a fungus can cause this strange growth.

wolf

A large, wild member of the dog family. It is found in cool forests in northern parts of the American continent and in parts of Europe. Wolves hunt in packs by night, and feed on other mammals, insects, molluscs and even fruit.

wombat

A small, bear-like marsupial with thick, coarse fur, found in Australia. It is a shy animal that hides in a burrow during the day.

woodpecker

A bird with a very strong beak for pecking wood. It has tough, stiff tail feathers to press against tree trunks and keep it upright as it climbs them. The woodpecker feeds on insects that it digs out of bark, and also digs holes in trees to nest in.

red-headed woodpecker

worm

A crawling, legless animal. The best known is the earthworm, which eats its way through soil. It is good for the soil, as it turns it over and lets air into it.

wren

A very small, brown bird with an upturned tail and a loud, clear song. It has short wings and cannot fly very far.

Xx

X-ray fish
A small freshwater fish found in South America. It gets its name because its bones show through its silvery, almost transparent body.

Yy

yellowhammer
A small, bright yellow perching bird with a chestnut back and rump. Its song is often described as 'a-little-bit-of-bread-and-no-cheese'.

yew
A coniferous tree with poisonous needles, bark and seeds. Its wood is often used for carving. Yew trees can live for over a thousand years.

Zz

zebra
A member of the horse family, found on grasslands and mountains in Africa, where it lives in large groups, or herds. Its white coat is heavily striped with black or dark brown. These stripes are as personal as human fingerprints, for no two zebras have exactly the same pattern.

zebu
A large greyish type of cattle found in Asia and Africa. It has big drooping ears and a hump on its back. The zebu thrives in hot climates, for it can keep its body temperature normal even in extreme heat.

zoology
The study of animal life.